The Official England Rugby
Annual 2010

Written By Martin Johnston

ENGLAND®
RUGBY

A Grange Publication

ISBN 978-1-906211-77-6

£6.99

CONTENTS

INTRODUCTION

Welcome to the Official England Rugby Annual 2010. We've got another bumper edition for you bursting with interesting info and pictures of all your favourite players.

It's been another eventful year for Martin Johnson and his England team with plenty to talk about. But we didn't stop there. There are also stacks of exclusive features on the important stuff like England Saxons, England Sevens and other England sides. There are in depth profiles of stars like Delon Armitage, Riki Flutey and Lee Mears. You'll also find out what the England boys get up to off the pitch. Who cooks a mean Spaghetti Carbonara? Who wanted to join the RAF? And who could have had a career as a street dancer? But that's just the fun side. For the serious stuff The Big England Quiz is back, bigger and better than ever, along with a cracking word search and some spot the ball pages. Enjoy!

MARTIN JOHNSON
SCHOOL REPORT 2009

AFTER HIS FIRST FULL SEASON IN CHARGE OF THE SENIOR SQUAD, WHAT WOULD ENGLAND LEGEND MARTIN JOHNSON'S SCHOOL REPORT FOR THE RFU LOOK LIKE? WE'VE MADE AN 'EDUCATED' GUESS!

After a tough start and a baptism of fire in the 2008 Investec Challenge Series, Martin has begun to re-establish England's reputation as a force to be reckoned with.

Definite signs of progress were detected during the RBS 6 Nations. Finishing runners-up and scoring the most tries is not to be sniffed at. But the highlight was clearly the stylish demolition of France at Twickenham.

The summer term brought more twists and turns. A predictably entertaining encounter with the Barbarians would have looked better as a win. Not many teams manage to beat Argentina by 22 points, so the 37-15 victory over the Pumas at Old Trafford was a real high point. A battling display was not enough to force victory in Salta in the return, so there is still plenty of work to do.

In terms of his players, some like Delon Armitage, Tom Croft and Matt Banahan have hit the ground running and added to the cohesion of what is clearly a tight knit squad. Great teams rely on even greater squads with a winning mentality. We firmly believe that Martin is beginning to grow and develop that squad and that under him England will regain the winning habit.

In his own words "It's been a difficult year in some ways, but we want to win test matches. There is not a 'Johnson way' of playing the game, we will play the way we need to play to win the match."

In summary, this has been a challenging year for Martin, but he has met those challenges well and is starting to build a squad that can do England proud again at the Rugby World Cup in New Zealand in 2011. We look forward to next term's matches with relish.

RBS 6 NATIONS 2009 ROUND UP

WEEKEND ONE

England laboured to a 36-11 victory over Italy with scrum half Harry Ellis scoring a try in each half, as Steffon Armitage made his debut alongside brother Delon. This was the first time England had fielded two siblings since Rory and Tony Underwood lined up on the wings in 1995. Elsewhere Ireland kicked off their campaign with a 30-21 win over France in Dublin and Wales beat Scotland 26-13 at Murrayfield.

WEEKEND TWO

In a packed and passionate Millennium Stadium, England out-scored the hosts on tries 2-1, with Paul Sackey and Delon Armitage going over. But Wales exploited English indiscipline and racked up six penalties as Mike Tindall and Andy Goode were both yellow-carded. In Paris, France edged out Scotland 22-13 and Ireland showed no mercy handing out a 38-9 pummelling to home side Italy in the Stadio Flaminio.

WEEKEND THREE

Poor discipline again left Martin Johnson wringing his hands in despair as Ireland sneaked a 14-13 victory over England at Croke Park. Harlequins scrum half Danny Care was the main culprit, being sin-binned 11 minutes before the end.

Full back Delon Armitage was the pick of the England players, latching on to a smart Andy Goode grubber to score a second consecutive try. Meanwhile France won their second home game in a row, beating Wales 21-16 and Scotland saw off Italy with a 26-6 home win.

While Ireland recorded their first Grand Slam in 61 years, England had a mixed RBS 6 Nations in 2009. The highlights were a scintillating 34-10 home victory over France, a runners-up finish and topping the try count with 16 but poor discipline led to consecutive defeats in Cardiff and Dublin.

WEEKEND FOUR

England finally showed what they were capable of under Martin Johnson, as they blew France away 34-10, scoring a try with their first attack and going on to score another four in the match. Riki Flutey scored two tries and Delon Armitage scored his third in as many matches. Wales narrowly beat an improving Italy 20-15 away and Ireland stayed on course for the Grand Slam by beating Scotland 22-15 at Murrayfield.

FINAL WEEKEND

On the final weekend, England regained the Calcutta Cup with a third straight home victory. They proved a little too strong for a determined Scotland side, recording a 26-12 win. Man of the match Riki Flutey added to tries by Ugo Monye and Mathew Tait and Danny Care weighed in with a drop goal. Ireland won the Grand Slam they'd been dreaming of for 61 years winning 17-15 in a tense and breathlessly close encounter with Wales at the Millennium Stadium. France ran riot in Rome beating Italy 50-8.

FINAL TABLE

	W	D	L	T	F	A	Pts
Ireland	5	0	0	12	121	73	10
England	3	0	2	16	124	70	6
France	3	0	2	14	124	101	6
Wales	3	0	2	8	100	81	6
Scotland	1	0	4	4	79	102	2
Italy	0	0	5	2	49	170	0

IN FOCUS:
DELON ARMITAGE

England Team Manager Martin Johnson called Delon Armitage's debut against the Pacific Islanders in November 2008 one of the best he'd ever seen and he has been first choice full back for England ever since, scoring tries right throughout 2009.

He began his rugby at Richmond at the age of eight before moving to France with his family. His career began to take shape at Racing Rugby Club de Nice although he was also playing football for Villeneuve Loubet. Fortunately he favoured rugby and was capped by France at U16 level but returned to England soon after.

On his return he joined the London Irish academy in 2002, going on to play for England U19s and England U21s. In 2004/5 he was named London Irish Young Player of the Season and was part of the England Sevens squad. Along with England team-mate Topsy Ojo, Delon has established himself as a prominent part of a truly threatening exiles backline, and his inclusion in the 2006 England Saxons squad for the Barclays Churchill Cup was just reward for some sparkling club performances that season.

As well as cementing his place as England's first choice full back, the 2008/9 season also saw him helping London Irish to a third place finish in the Guinness Premiership and a Grand Final spot at Twickenham, where they lost narrowly, 10-9 to Leicester Tigers.

Delon's personal rewards for a superb season saw him nominated for Player of the Year awards for the Guinness Premiership and the PRA, as well as a nomination for Player of the Tournament for the RBS 6 Nations.

DID YOU KNOW?

Delon's stepfather John played rugby for Hatfield RFC and did such a good job encouraging his sons' development in the game, that three of them are now professional players. Steffon is with Delon at London Irish and is also a member of the England squad while Bevon is with National One club Doncaster Knights. Delon was the first native West Indian to play rugby union for England and also enjoys cricket, tennis and the Playstation. He and girlfriend Jemma have three young children.

Delon Armitage made the giant leap from being a great prospect to becoming a fully fledged member of the England squad with a dazzling debut against the Pacific Islanders. He went on to make the full back berth his own during the RBS 6 Nations in 2009.

CLUB: LONDON IRISH

POSITION: FULL BACK/CENTRE

BORN: 15.12.83 | SAN FERNANDO, TRINIDAD

HEIGHT: 1.85 (6'1")

WEIGHT: 93KG (14ST 10LB)

REPRESENTATIVE HONOURS: ENGLAND U19S, ENGLAND U21S (2004 WORLD CHAMPIONSHIPS), ENGLAND SAXONS (2006 BARCLAYS CHURCHILL CUP, 2007 BARCLAYS CHURCHILL CUP V USA), ENGLAND SEVENS (2005 SINGAPORE, PARIS)

CAPS: 11

POINTS: 34 – 5T, DG, 2P

INTERNATIONAL RECORD: 2008 PI, A, SA, NZ 2009 IT, W, I, F, S, A (1,2)

SPOT THE DIFFERENCE

LOOK AT THE PICTURE BELOW, CAN YOU SPOT 6 DIFFERENCES BETWEEN THE TWO LINEUPS? (Answers on page 61)

THE ENGLAND RUGBY QUIZ

1. Delon Armitage played for France U16s. True or False?
2. Which club does England hooker Lee Mears play for?
3. Where will the 2011 Rugby World Cup be held?
4. Who is England's record points scorer?
5. Who would England need to beat to complete a 'Triple Crown'?
6. Which club does England flanker Tom Croft play for?
7. Who captained England in the 2009 RBS 6 Nations?
8. Scotland won the 2009 Calcutta Cup match against England. True or False?
9. Which England player came off the bench to score a drop goal in that match against Scotland?
10. England hooker Dylan Hartley was born in Australia. True or False?
11. In which city did England win the Rugby World Cup final in 2003?
12. England scored the most tries in the RBS 6 Nations 2009. How many?
13. How many times have England played in the Rugby World Cup final?
14. Which club does England winger Mark Cueto play for?
15. Who won the 2009 Guinness Premiership Grand Final?
16. Which former England full back took over as head coach of Sale Sharks in 2009?
17. Twickenham used to be referred to as 'The Cabbage Patch'. True or False?
18. Which team won the 2009 EDF Energy Cup at Twickenham?
19. Where was the 2009 IRB Rugby World Cup Sevens tournament held?
20. Who captained England in the 2007 Rugby World Cup final?

Answers on page 61

Kids love ENGLAND RUGBY

JSC
England Rugby Junior Supporters Club

Surprise them with a JSC membership today!

ENGLAND'S GREATEST EVER MATCHES

THE FIRST EVER WIN

SCORE LINE: England 8 Scotland 3
WHERE: The Oval, London
WHEN: 1872

Great because: This was England's first ever win. It was their second ever game and great revenge for having been beaten 4-1 by the Scots the previous year in the world's first ever rugby international. That game took place at Raeburn Place in Edinburgh, but England made no mistake in the return match at what is now the home of Surrey CCC.

THE HARDEST FOUGHT

SCORE LINE: France 10 England 19
WHERE: Parc des Princes, Paris
WHEN: October 19 1991

Great because: In the second Rugby World Cup in 1991, host nation England had come second in their group after losing to New Zealand in the first match. This meant a showdown with France at their spiritual home, Parc des Princes, if they were to progress to the semi finals. There was no love lost between the two teams in those days and this one was not for the faint hearted. England hooker that day, Brian Moore said "It was ferocious, probably the most physical game I ever played in." When the dust had settled England had won 19-10 thanks to tries from Rory Underwood and Will Carling plus the boot of Jonathan Webb.

THE GREATEST DAY

SCORE LINE: Australia 17 England 20
WHERE: Telstra Stadium, Sydney
WHEN: November 22 2003

Great because: England's greatest day in rugby came in the final of the 2003 Rugby World Cup, a match which has already passed into English sporting folklore. It's the only time that a northern hemisphere team has won the world cup. Despite going behind to an early Lote Tuqiri try, England showed the resolve that had made Clive Woodward's team the best in the world that year. A try from Jason Robinson and that drop goal from Jonny Wilkinson floored the Aussies in their own back yard and an ecstatic Martin Johnson lifted the William Webb Ellis Cup.

IN FOCUS:
LEE MEARS

Lee Mears started playing rugby in his home town of Torquay in Devon, playing for the minis at Torquay Athletic and went on to play for the first XV of nearby Paignton College. He then moved to the famous rugby powerhouse of Colston's School in Bristol coming under the tutelage of Alan Martinovic and former England head coach Andy Robinson.

He represented England at U16, U18 and U19 Colts level and in 1997 was a member of the now famous, unbeaten England U18 Schools party. That team toured Australia and included fellow World Cup squad members Jonny Wilkinson, Andrew Sheridan and England captain, Steve Borthwick. They won the Grand Slam and dished out hidings the length and breadth of Australia on an eight match tour, during which they scored almost 550 points and conceded just 62. Lee also played for the U21s in three IRB World Championship matches in New Zealand.

He progressed to England A and appeared in two consecutive Churchill Cup tournaments in 2004 and 2005. He first played for the full England side when he came on as a replacement for Steve Thompson against Samoa in 2005 but it took until 2008 for him to finally shrug off his 'bench warmer' tag and become England's first choice hooker.

He has spent all his professional career with Bath and captained them at the Middlesex Sevens at Twickenham in 2006. In 2009 he signed a deal to keep him at The Recreation Ground for at least another four years.

DID YOU KNOW?

Lee would have joined the RAF had he not opted for rugby and he is currently learning to fly. An Aston Villa fan, his rugby hero as a youngster was former Bath hooker Graham Dawe. Lee loves to cook for himself and his wife Danielle and has even taken culinary courses to develop his repertoire.

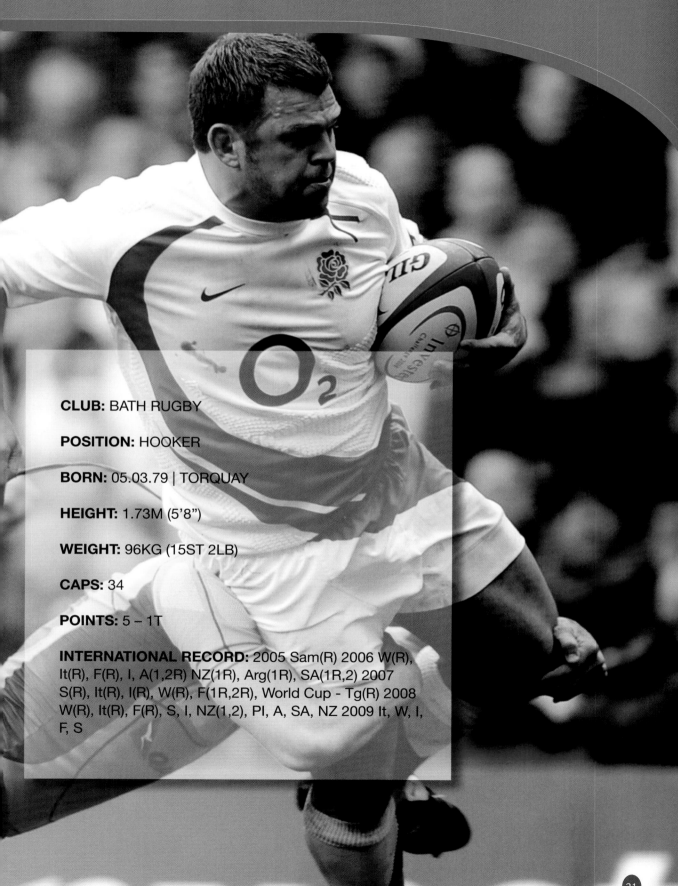

A product of mini rugby in his home town of Torquay, Lee Mears also played for the all-conquering Colston's School team under the guidance of Andy Robinson. The England hooker has spent the whole of his professional career at Bath.

CLUB: BATH RUGBY

POSITION: HOOKER

BORN: 05.03.79 | TORQUAY

HEIGHT: 1.73M (5'8")

WEIGHT: 96KG (15ST 2LB)

CAPS: 34

POINTS: 5 – 1T

INTERNATIONAL RECORD: 2005 Sam(R) 2006 W(R), It(R), F(R), I, A(1,2R) NZ(1R), Arg(1R), SA(1R,2) 2007 S(R), It(R), I(R), W(R), F(1R,2R), World Cup - Tg(R) 2008 W(R), It(R), F(R), S, I, NZ(1,2), PI, A, SA, NZ 2009 It, W, I, F, S

BEN FODEN

Chester-born Ben Foden made his England debut in the 2009 RBS 6 Nations as a replacement against Italy and kept his place in the squad for the game against the Barbarians.

He earned his call-up on the back of some outstanding displays as both scrum half and full back for Northampton. He joined the Saints in summer 2008 after spending four frustrating years at Sale Sharks, where he had graduated from the Sale academy Jets squad. At Franklin's Gardens he linked up again with his former England U21s coach Jim Mallinder, who gave him the opportunity to play in both positions.

Ben was a member of the 2006 Grand Slam-winning England U21s squad, playing in all five matches and scoring three tries. He also scored a try on his debut for England Saxons in last June's Barclay's Churchill Cup.

In 2009 he capped an excellent season for Northampton Saints by collecting the PRA's Young Player of the Year Award.

DID YOU KNOW?
Ben likes to sing and his nickname is 'Pop Idol' because, when he was 18, he entered the TV show of that name. He had been a singer in a band called Anonymous when he was 13. His Bromsgrove School teacher, Paul Mullan, was a big influence on his career, as was his Dad Rob, who coached Ben's youth team and now coaches Chester RFC.

Club: Northampton Saints
Position: Scrum half/Full back
Born: 22.07.85 | Chester
Height: 1.83m (6' 0")

Weight: 94kg (14st 12lb)

Representative honours: Cheshire & North of England U16s, England A U16s, England U19s, England Counties, England U21s (2005 6 Nations v W, F, I, It, S) World Championships v W, It, S, F, I , 2006 6 Nations and World Championships, England Sevens (2006/7 Dub, George, Well, San D, Adelaide, 2007/08 Dub, George), England Saxons (2008 Barclays Churchill Cup v USA, I(R), S(R))

Caps: 1
Points: 0
International record: 2009 It(R)

OLLY MORGAN

Millfield-educated Olly Morgan has had more than his fair share of injuries in recent years including a dislocated shoulder, concussion, a burst blood vessel in a thigh muscle that needed hospital treatment and a fractured finger. However he had a great season for Gloucester in 2009 and is now back in England contention.

He made an unexpected debut in 2007, when he was due to feature for England Saxons against Italy A. However an injury to Iain Balshaw meant he was called up for his senior debut against Scotland in the RBS 6 Nations. He kept his place for the next match against Ireland at Croke Park, but was unlucky to last only 30 minutes before getting injured.

He started his international career with the England U16s in 2001, won eight caps for England U19s in 2003 and played in the Young England Sevens team in 2004. He went on to make his debut for the U21s against Wales in Newport in 2005.

His return to form for the Cherry and Whites in the 2008/9 season saw him named as full back in the Sky Sports-nominated Guinness Premiership Dream Team.

Club: Gloucester Rugby
Position: Full back
Born: 03.11.85 | London
Height: 1.88m (6' 2")

Weight: 95kg (14st 13lb)

Representative honours: England U16s (2001), England U19s (2002/3, 2004 World Championship), Young England 7s (2004), England U21s (2005 6 Nations and World Championship, 2006 6 Nations)

Caps: 2
Points: 0
International record: 2007 S, I

DID YOU KNOW?
Olly's father Paul played for England Schools and his Grandfather was an Oxford Blue at rugby.

Olly is very much an all-rounder and also represented England U16s at hockey, he is also an accomplished scuba diver and snowboarder.

Club: London Wasps
Position: Lock
Born: 03.12.82 | Warrington
Height: 1.98m (6'6")

Weight: 111kg (17st 6lb)

Representative honours: England U18s, England Saxons (2008 6 Nations v I(R); 2008 Barclays Churchill Cup v USA, I, S)

International record: Uncapped

GEORGE SKIVINGTON

George Skivington is a mobile, attacking lock very much in the mould of his one-time hero, All Black legend Ian Jones. Born in Warrington, he first joined the Saracens academy but transferred to his current club, London Wasps in 2003.

He made his first team debut in August 2003 against Stade Francais and went on to make several more senior appearances, while captaining the Wasps A team in the 2004/5 season. In 2005/6 he made 19 more appearances for the first team and would have cemented his place as a regular, had a problematic toe injury not kept him on the sidelines.

Despite the next season also being plagued with injury he still helped inspire the A team win their league and made 16 more appearances for the first XV.

George made his England Saxons debut as a replacement against Ireland A in February 2008. He celebrated his first start by scoring a try in a 64-10 victory over the USA in the opening round of the 2008 Barclays Churchill Cup in Ottawa, Canada. He was named captain of the team to play Ireland A at Donnybrook in February 2009 but the match was called off at the last minute due to a frozen pitch. Injury again kept him out of England Saxons' summer tour squad in 2009.

DID YOU KNOW?
George reckons that as most of his mates are in the construction trade, if he hadn't made it as a rugby player, he would probably be a builder. A keen footballer at school he cites travelling and listening to music as his hobbies.

Club: Gloucester Rugby
Position: Fly half
Born: 18.05.86 | Gloucester
Height: 1.75m (5' 8")

Weight: 80kg (12st 5lb)

Representative honours: England A U16 (2001/2), England U18 (2002/3), 2004 Sevens Commonwealth Youth Games, Australia (silver medallists), England U19s (2004 6 Nations, 2005 6 Nations, World Championship, Durban), England U21s (2006 6 Nations and World Championships), England Saxons (2007 Barclays Churchill Cup v USA; 2008 Barclays Churchill Cup v USA, I, S)

International record: Uncapped

RYAN LAMB

Ryan Lamb's first sporting success came as a primary school footballer with Gloucester City FC but he is now considered one of England's most promising young fly halves. After attending Severn Vale and St Peter's High School in Gloucester he made the switch to rugby and joined Spartans RUFC.

An accomplished goal-kicker, he joined his home club on professional terms in 2001 and is currently a leading member of coach Dean Ryan's hotly-tipped young first team squad.

In 2005 he was a member of the England U19s squad that made it to the semi-finals of the IRB World Championships, losing to hosts and eventual winners South Africa. A year later he was voted man of the match for the U21s against Italy and became a key member of the 2006 squad. He notched up 37 points as England won the Grand Slam in the 5 Nations and another 15 at the IRB U21 World Championships.
He made his debut for England Saxons on his 21st birthday, marking it with another man of the match performance against the USA.

DID YOU KNOW?
Ryan professes to be a big Manchester United fan and greatly admires Wayne Rooney for achieving so much at such a young age.

IN FOCUS:
RIKI FLUTEY

After qualifying on the grounds of residency, Maori flyer Riki Flutey was finally persuaded to play for England by All Black legend Norm Hewitt and has already made a massive impact on Martin Johnson's side.

He made his debut in the centre alongside London Wasps team mate Danny Cipriani in the autumn of 2008 in a 39-13 win over the Pacific Islanders at Twickenham. He went on to keep his place for the series and played against Australia, South Africa and New Zealand.

He had a hugely impressive debut tournament in the 2009 RBS 6 Nations, scoring two tries against France and one each against Italy and Scotland. Riki started playing rugby as a scrum half and represented New Zealand at various levels of 'age grade' rugby, the crowning moment of which was winning the IRB U19 World Championship in 1999. He then switched to fly half for New Zealand U21s.

He arrived in England in 2005 from Wellington Hurricanes having also been called up by New Zealand Maori along the way. He scored 15 tries and racked up 272 points in his first two seasons with London Irish but was snapped up by London Wasps in 2007. He won the Guinness Premiership with them and was voted the PRA Computacentre Player's Player of the year in 2008.

Prior to his inclusion in the England squad, he explained: "I spoke to family members and they were right behind me. The Guinness Premiership has enabled me to nail down one position instead of being a utility back and I said if the chance came to play for England, I'd grab it."

DID YOU KNOW?
Outside rugby Riki is passionate about music. He sings and plays the guitar and particularly enjoys karaoke. He has an older brother called Mano, who has also played at every New Zealand age grade and also has another brother and three sisters.

Maori Riki Flutey scored 272 points in his first two seasons in English club rugby. Nobody was surprised when after qualifying through residency, he was called up by Martin Johnson to become England's first choice at Inside Centre.

CLUB: AC BRIVE, FRANCE

POSITION: CENTRE

BORN: 10.02.80 | WAIRARAPA, NEW ZEALAND

HEIGHT: 1.79M (5' 11")

WEIGHT: 93KG (14ST 10LB)

REPRESENTATIVE HONOURS: NEW ZEALAND U19S, NEW ZEALAND U21S, NEW ZEALAND MAORI

CAPS: 9

POINTS: 20 – 4T

INTERNATIONAL RECORD: 2008 PI, A, SA, NZ 2009 IT, W, I, F, S

IN FOCUS:
DYLAN HARTLEY

Dylan Hartley was born in the famous rugby town of Rotorua, scene of many famous victories for the Maori and other New Zealand representative sides over various touring teams.

Having been steeped in the Maori rugby tradition he is known for his soft hands and quick thinking, bringing all the skills of a centre and the traditional aggression of a front row forward to his game.

He learnt his rugby at Rotorua Boys High School and played a handful of games for Bay of Plenty U18s before moving to England as a teenager. In those days he was a prop but became a hooker at Northampton Saints, his current club. The initial experiment proved so successful that England international hooker Steve Thompson was often forced to play out of position as a flanker.

While staying with relatives in Crowborough, West Sussex in 2003, Dylan was called up by an enterprising England U18s management team, having qualified by English ancestry. He returned home to New Zealand shortly after but jumped at the chance to come back and play for England U19s.

After an impressive series of games for the U19s, he was quickly drafted into the England U21 squad, where despite being only 19, he provided cover for all three front row positions at the IRB World Championships in Argentina.

He initially signed professional terms for Worcester but transferred to Northampton in the summer of 2005. He made 16 appearances in his debut season, including a baptism of fire as hooker against Leicester Tigers.

Dylan's impressive form in his debut season in the Guinness Premiership earned him a call up to the England Saxons squad for the 2007 6 Nations. He continued to catch the eye, scoring tries against Italy A and Ireland A.

He has continued to blossom under the guidance of former England hooker Dorian West at Northampton Saints. Dylan has also worked with specialist coach Steve Peters who helped British cyclists Bradley Wiggins and Victoria Pendleton win Gold medals in Beijing.

DID YOU KNOW?
On a visit home to New Zealand in 2005, Dylan bought a ticket for the British and Irish Lions match with his old side, Bay of Plenty. But the night before the game he received a call from Nigel Redman telling him England Under 21s in Argentina needed him. He was on the next plane and missed the Lions game. It was while he was in South America that he converted to playing hooker for the first time.

Like Rikki Flutey, New Zealand-born Dylan Hartley chose England over the possibility of playing for the All Blacks. The combative hooker continues to push Lee Mears hard to be England's first choice Number 2.

CLUB: NORTHAMPTON SAINTS

POSITION: HOOKER

BORN: 24.03.86 | ROTORUA, NEW ZEALAND

HEIGHT: 1.86 (6' 1")

WEIGHT: 109KG (17ST 3LB)

CAPS: 11

POINTS: 0

INTERNATIONAL RECORD: 2008 PI(R), A(R), SA(R), NZ(R) 2009 IT(R), W(R), I(R), F(R), S(R), A (1,2)

REPRESENTATIVE ENGLAND TEAMS

You know Martin Johnson's side is building nicely towards the Rugby World Cup in 2011 and you probably know that England has a very strong Sevens side and that the side previously known as England A takes the field these days as England Saxons.

But did you know that England has many other representative sides? And that most of Johnno's squad will have first pulled on an England shirt for one of them? As well as England Saxons, there are England age group teams at Under 20, Under 18 and Under 16 levels as well as an England Students team. There is also an England Counties XV and an England Deaf team. In 2009 England Under 20s firmly established themselves as the number two side in the world behind New Zealand after losing to the All Blacks in the final of the IRB Toshiba Junior World Championships in Japan.

The highlight of the season was probably their 40-21 semi-final win over South Africa. James Gaskell of Sale Sharks, Rory Clegg of Harlequins and Tom Homer of London Irish all had excellent seasons and will be available to the squad again in 2010.

England Under 18s had an even better season, culminating in a grand slam win of the Five Nations Festival. Captain Alex Gray (Barnard Castle School and Newcastle Falcons) and George Ford (Rishworth School and Leicester Tigers) were the pick of the bunch from a very impressive squad. England Students also impressed in 2009 winning all their games, including a stunning second half comeback to secure victory over the French at Clifton RFC. Loughborough University's Grant Pointer scored all England's points that day and made a major contribution in every match.

For the England Counties XV 2009 was all about exciting experiences. They made their debut at Twickenham, losing to a very strong French Amateur side and in the summer enjoyed a highly successful tour of Japan and South Korea. They recorded their highest ever win on that tour, beating the Korean President's XV 108-10.

The England Deaf team lost their only game of 2009, 55-10 to Wales, who retained the Broadstreet Cup, but there were a lot of good signs for an England side fielding 10 new caps.

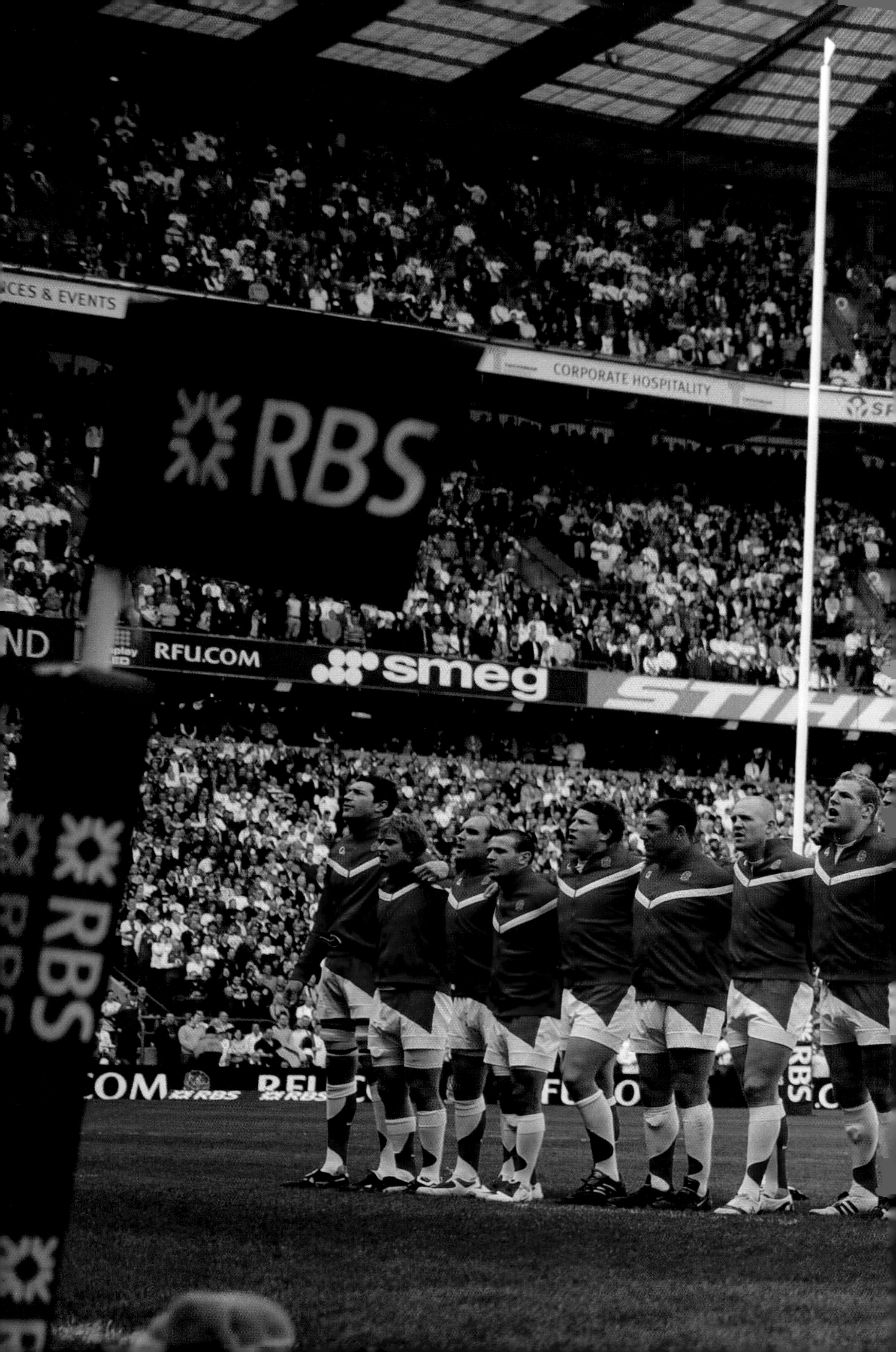

RBS
CORPORATE HOSPITALITY
RFU.COM
smeg
RBS

DOWNTIME
WHAT THE ENGLAND PLAYERS GET UP TO OFF THE FIELD

MY HERO!

England players seem to have a healthy respect for their All Black counterparts, as this list of their heroes shows:

DANNY CARE: JONAH LOMU
RIKI FLUTEY: JOE STANLEY
DELON ARMITAGE: JERRY COLLINS
GEORGE SKIVINGTON: IAN JONES

COME DINE WITH ME

England hooker Lee Mears has taken courses to improve his culinary skills and flanker Tom Croft is very proud of his Spaghetti Carbonara but dinner at Danny Care's would probably be the most fun as he lists his ideal dinner guests as Alan Partridge, David Beckham and Jessica Alba!

IF I WASN'T A RUGBY PLAYER, I WOULD PROBABLY BE....

...Steve Borthwick: **in finance**
...Matthew Tait: **studying to be a doctor or a vet**
...George Chuter: **teacher**
...Andy Goode: **professional cricketer**
...Lee Mears: **RAF pilot**
...Julian White: **a sheep farmer**
  (mainly because I already am!)

THE BEAUTIFUL GAME

Like most of us the England rugby players also enjoy football. Delon Armitage played for Villeneuve-Loubet as a youngster in France and Dan Hipkiss played for Suffolk U13s before turning to rugby. Ben Kay is a big Liverpool supporter and no doubt enjoys some banter with Manchester United fans, Richard Wigglesworth and Ryan Lamb and Arsenal fan, Jordan Turner-Hall.

IN FOCUS:
DANNY CARE

Yorkshire terrier Danny Care started his rugby at Prince Henry's Grammar School in Otley, when his Year 8 side were crowned as Yorkshire Cup winners. He made the natural progression to play for his local club, Otley and then turned professional a few miles up the road with Leeds Tykes.

After representing England at U16 and U18 levels he became part of a highly successful U19s set-up which played in the Sevens tournament at the Commonwealth Youth Games in Australia in 2004 and went on to finish third at the 2006 IRB U19 World Championship in Dubai, England's highest ever finish in that tournament.

2006 must have been an exhausting year as Danny also won a Silver medal as a member of the England Sevens team at the Commonwealth Games in Melbourne and was part of the England U21s squad at the IRB World Championships.

The next season, 2007/8 his leadership qualities were recognised as he captained England U20s in all five of their 6 Nations games. He also made his debut for England Saxons in a 38-15 victory over Italy in Ragusa.

He made his first start for the senior team in 2008 as part of the squad touring New Zealand that summer. His big break came in the first test in Auckland where he was a second half replacement for Richard Wigglesworth. He went one better a week later and made his first start in an England shirt in the second test in Christchurch. He caught the eye by scoring from his own tap penalty that day and kept his place as starting scrum half in all four games of the Investec Challenge Series in November that year.

In 2009 Danny was a replacement in three of England's RBS 6 Nations matches and managed a classy drop goal in the Calcutta Cup victory over Scotland. He went on to start both matches against the Pumas in June. He also enjoyed an excellent season for his club Harlequins and was nominated for the PRA's Young Player of the Year Award.

DID YOU KNOW?
Danny played football at the Sheffield Wednesday FC academy for three years, and he also enjoys playing tennis and snooker in his spare time. His nickname is DC, he lists Matt Dawson and Jonah Lomu as his rugby heroes and his most prized possessions are his England caps. His dinner guest wish list includes David Beckham, Alan Partridge and Jessica Alba and says he'd make them all eat his favourite food, fish and chips.

Scrum half Danny Care has represented England at nine different levels since being picked for the U16s. He scored from his own tap penalty to score a try against the All Blacks in Christchurch on his first full start in 2008.

CLUB: HARLEQUINS

POSITION: SCRUM HALF

BORN: 02.01.87 | LEEDS

HEIGHT: 1.74M (5'8")

WEIGHT: 84KG (13ST 4LB)

REPRESENTATIVE HONOURS: ENGLAND U16S, ENGLAND U18S, ENGLAND U19 SEVENS; COMMONWEALTH YOUTH GAMES AUSTRALIA 2004, ENGLAND SEVENS (2005/6 WELLINGTON & LOS ANGELES, COMMONWEALTH GAMES SILVER MEDAL, 2006/7 SEVENS SERIES – HONG KONG, ADELAIDE, LONDON, EDINBURGH, 2007/8 WELLINGTON), ENGLAND U19S (2006 6 NATIONS, 2006 IRB U19 WORLD CHAMPIONSHIPS, DUBAI), ENGLAND U21S (2006 U21 WORLD CHAMPIONSHIPS), ENGLAND U20S (2007 6 NATIONS), ENGLAND SAXONS (2008 V IT (R), F (R), S (R))

CAPS: 11

POINTS: 8 – 1T, DG

INTERNATIONAL RECORD: 2008 NZ (1R, 2), PI, A, SA, NZ 2009 I(R), F(R), S(R), A (1,2)

SPOT THE BALL

ANSWERS ON PAGE 61

WORDSEARCH

How good are you at finding hidden words? You'll need all your skills
to find and circle the 20 rugby-related words we've hidden in our wordsearch
below. Remember, the words can be vertical, horizontal, backwards or diagonal...

```
J  B  E  F  D  D  R  O  P  G  O  A  L  T
O  N  F  I  J  L  I  N  E  O  U  T  E  O
H  F  L  Y  H  A  L  F  S  E  B  S  E  U
N  L  U  Z  J  E  E  G  G  O  P  A  Q  C
S  Z  T  L  N  X  L  A  T  S  C  X  N  H
O  B  E  H  O  R  T  E  N  C  K  O  E  J
N  A  Y  B  G  I  U  A  B  R  A  N  N  U
K  N  D  T  M  C  E  K  S  U  Y  S  G  D
P  A  E  R  R  R  Y  N  X  M  E  L  L  G
C  H  A  M  T  Y  E  T  K  H  L  I  A  E
R  A  N  N  E  V  L  Y  E  A  L  G  N  X
O  N  E  M  E  A  T  I  N  L  I  Z  D  A
F  C  P  S  V  E  R  J  N  F  S  F  E  M
T  Y  W  L  I  O  N  S  P  E  C  Q  C  K
```

LINE OUT	SCRUM HALF	JOHNSON	CROFT	SEVENS
TRY LINE	CENTRE	FLUTEY	ELLIS	SAXONS
TOUCH JUDGE	FLY HALF	BANAHAN	KAY	ENGLAND
DROP GOAL	MEARS	ARMITAGE	CUETO	LIONS

PRIDE OF THE LIONS

The British and Irish Lions tour to South Africa in 2009 was undoubtedly a roaring success. The three test matches reached a level of intensity unique in world rugby and no quarter was asked or given.

Despite England flanker Tom Croft scoring two tries in the first test in Durban, the Lions lost 26-21 to the home side and left themselves a mountain to climb to win the series.

The second test at Loftus Versfeld in Pretoria was a battle royale with both sides desperate for the win. Unfortunately the Lions suffered a second defeat, going down 28-25, losing in the last minute to a long range penalty from Morne Steyn.

However, they returned to form in some style, romping home 28-9 in the last test at Ellis Park in Cape Town. England winger Ugo Monye found the victory particularly sweet after being dropped following the first Test defeat in Durban. A relieved and emotional Harlequins winger said of that try: "I almost cried when I put the ball down - to look up and see all the Lions supporters was amazing. It was a long tour but I loved every minute of it. It's been a great honour to have worn and won in, a Lions Test jersey."

Monye, Riki Flutey and Tom Croft may be relative newcomers to the international stage but even for a veteran like Phil Vickery it was a remarkable end to a memorable tour. "South Africa deserved their series win but we came home with our heads held high," said Vickery. "I just hope that Lions tours will continue because this has been very special for me."

Other highlights for the England contingent were Simon Shaw's masterful Lions test debut (at last!) and Andrew Sheridan's taming of the hitherto unstoppable Tendai Mtawarira in Durban.

They may have lost the Test series against South Africa but England's British Lions returned home in the summer with their heads held high.

41

GUESS WHO?

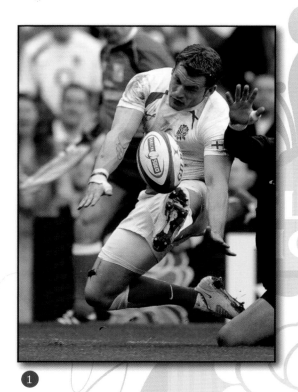

1

2

3

4

ANSWERS ON PAGE 61

ENGLAND SAXONS
CHURCHILL CUP 2009 ROUND UP

England Saxons showed every sign that they would retain the Churchill Cup for a third straight year in 2009, but fell short at the final hurdle.

Ably captained by Newcastle Falcons' flanker Phil Dowson and Bath Rugby's Stuart Hooper and coached by Stuart Lancaster they beat Argentina Jaguars 28-20 in the first game at Infinity Park in Denver, Colorado.

They went on to beat the hosts USA, 56-17 at the same venue to book their passage to the final with Northampton Saints' Stephen Myler turning in a Man of the Match performance and notching 21 points. Saracens' Noah Cato scored the pick of seven tries.

Unfortunately they came up against a very strong Ireland A pack firing on all cylinders and lost 49-22 at Dick's Sporting Good's Park in Denver. The Irish scored six tries to England's two and were good value for their win over a stunned Saxons side. Winger Tom Varndell

and flanker Ben Woods (both Leicester Tigers) scored the tries and Myler kicked four penalties. Unfortunately Woods was also sin binned, giving his team a mountain to climb in the last period of the game. Skipper Dowson was shell shocked afterwards and admitted "We took a pasting". He went on to say "There are no excuses. It wasn't a pretty sight at all. We just didn't look after our ball, whereas Ireland did. We didn't work hard enough at the breakdown and we have learned some harsh lessons. We have to go away and look at the videos but we just were not good enough today."

Head coach Lancaster was equally blunt "At this level there are no second chances. Our desire was there but our execution wasn't." So the Saxons season ended in frustration but plenty of players shone through to give Martin Johnson and the selectors something to think about in 2010. Myler and Dowson could be knocking on the door, along with Gloucester's Luke Narraway and Newcastle Falcons' scrum half Micky Young.

IN FOCUS:
TOM CROFT

England flanker Tom Croft is well known for his speed and is one of the quickest forwards in both the England and Leicester Tigers' squads. A former pupil of Park House School in Newbury and well known rugby school Oakham, he began his senior career at Newbury RFC in National League One, where he played for five years.

He moved to Welford Road in 2004 and was named Leicester Tigers Academy Player of the Year in his first season, making his Guinness Premiership debut the next season against Gloucester.

He began the next season, 2006/7, as the star of the Middlesex Sevens, scoring five tries in four games, which took Tigers to the final that year. He went on to make 13 first team appearances, scoring three tries, including a spectacular long-range finish in the EDF Energy Cup final against the Ospreys.

He began his representative rugby with the South of England 18 Group in 2002 and by 2006 had progressed to play for England U21s, winning a man of the match award in his first game against Wales and helping the team to a Grand Slam. The next season his fearsome pace also helped secure a win for England Saxons over New Zealand Maori in the 2007 Barclays Churchill Cup.

He made his full England debut as a replacement for the injured James Haskell in the 24-13 victory over France in the 2008 RBS 6 Nations and started the next game against Scotland. His form in the 2009 RBS 6 Nations was so good it was no surprise when he was named as one of the English contingent to tour South Africa with the British & Irish Lions.

DID YOU KNOW?
Tom enjoys cooking and usually has spaghetti carbonara the night before a game. He attributes some of his agility to being a former member of the West Berkshire Youth Dance Group in which he studied contemporary, modern and street dance.

A Lion and a Tiger, Tom Croft was named Man of the Match in England's best showing of the 2009 RBS 6 Nations, a 34-10 victory over France. The Leicester flanker is a former student of street dance, now putting his agility to good use on the rugby field.

CLUB: LEICESTER TIGERS
POSITION: FLANKER
BORN: 07.11.85 | BASINGSTOKE
HEIGHT: 1.98M (6'6")

WEIGHT: 105KG (16ST 7LB)

REPRESENTATIVE HONOURS: SOUTH OF ENGLAND, ENGLAND 18 GROUP (2002-2004), ENGLAND U21S (2006 U21 6 NATIONS AND IRB U21 WORLD CHAMPIONSHIPS), ENGLAND SEVENS (2006-7 WIDER SQUAD), ENGLAND SAXONS (2007 BARCLAYS CHURCHILL CUP)

CAPS: 13

POINTS: 0

INTERNATIONAL RECORD: 2008 F(R), S, I, NZ(2R), PI, A, SA(R), NZ(R), 2009 IT(R), W(R), I(R), F, S

ALEXANDER 'PRINCE' OBLENSKY
1936
Position: Wing

Although he only played one season for England, 'Prince' Oblensky's place in English rugby folklore was sealed when he scored two tries on his debut, a 13-0 win over New Zealand. It was the first time England had beaten the All Blacks and Oblensky's second try, captured for posterity by Pathe News, saw him run half the length of the field and beat several opposition players. At the time (1936) it was widely regarded as the greatest try ever scored. A genuine Prince of the Russian Rurik dynasty, he was a naturalised Englishman who died when his Hurricane fighter crashed while he was serving for the RAF in World War II.

CLIVE WOODWARD
1980-1984
Position: Centre
Also: Head Coach

Although best known as the architect of England's Rugby World Cup win in 2003, Clive Woodward was a very successful player in his day. He played his club rugby with Harlequins then Leicester- where he formed a famous partnership with Paul Dodge- and later in his career with Manly. He gained 21 caps and scored 16 points and was well known for favouring an expansive style, which yielded some spectacular tries. He also toured twice with the British and Irish Lions.

Last year we named England's most capped player Jason Leonard, highest scorer Jonny Wilkinson and World Cup-winning skipper Martin Johnson as well as legends Bill Beaumont, Wavell Wakefield and Rory Underwood in our Hall of Fame. Here are four more of England's best ever...

ROB ANDREW
1985-1997
Position: Fly Half
Also: Head Coach,
Director of Elite Rugby

The RFU's current Director of Elite Rugby was also an outstanding player in his day with 71 caps and 396 points to his name. He made his England debut in 1985 against Romania at Twickenham and went on to win 3 Grand Slams and play in consecutive Rugby World Cups. Perhaps best known as a player for the last minute drop goal which beat Australia at the Rugby World Cup in 1995, he also holds England's record for most points scored in an international (30 against Canada) and played first class cricket for Combined Universities.

JEREMY GUSCOTT
1989-1999
Position: Centre

Considered by many pundits to be one of the best outside centres ever to play the game Jeremy Guscott was called "The Prince of Centres" by Clive Woodward. Born in Bath he remained loyal to his home club for the whole of his career, making his debut in 1984 and scoring 710 points. His first game for England against Romania in Bucharest in 1989, yielded a hat-trick of tries and he was fast-tracked into the British and Irish Lions for that year's tour of Australia, where he made an immediate impact. He went on to play for the Lions again in New Zealand in 1993 and scored a famous match-winning drop goal against South Africa in 1997. He gained 65 England caps and scored 143 points and is now a well-known BBC TV presenter.

Despite a relatively poor showing in the Rugby World Cup Sevens in Dubai, England had another successful Sevens season in 2009. They won two of the IRB World Series events and finished third in the table behind Fiji and South Africa.

But arguably the finest achievement was England captain Ollie Phillips being named IRB Sevens Player of the Year. The Newcastle Falcons winger is a Sevens specialist, he led his club to victory in the 2008 Middlesex Sevens before leading England in last season's campaign. "It's been a fantastic year personally and collectively for our team and to captain any England side is a huge honour." he said after receiving the award from Scottish legend Gavin Hastings at Murrayfield.

England's two IRB tournament scalps came with their first ever win in Wellington, New Zealand and a dramatic victory on home soil at Twickenham.

That win in the Emirates Airline London Sevens came courtesy of a thrilling 31-26 triumph over New

Zealand in a classic final that went to sudden death extra time. England staged a magnificent second half comeback after trailing 19-0 at the interval to tries by Kurt Baker and two from Julian Savea, with Uche Oduoza, Micky Young and James Rodwell all going over to level the score for the home side. The All Blacks wrested back the lead with a try from Zar Lawrence only for England's Dan Norton to score a last minute try which Ben Gollings converted to make the match 26-26.

Cometh the hour cometh the man, Newcastle Falcon Micky Young sealed England's victory with the 'golden try', sending the sun-kissed Twickenham crowd home very happy. It was also a special day for veteran campaigner Ben Gollings. His three conversions in the final took him to 2000 career points in the IRB Sevens World Series, which makes him all time top scorer ahead of Fiji's Waisale Serevi, who scored 1310 points.

DELON ARMITAGE

Club: London Irish
Position: Full Back/centre
Born: 15.12.83
Birthplace: San Fernando, Trinidad

Height: 1.85m
Weight: 93kg
Caps: 11
Points: 34 – 5T,DG,2P

STEFFON ARMITAGE

Club: London Irish
Position: Flanker
Born: 20.09.85
Birthplace: San Fernando, Trinidad

Height: 1.75m
Weight: 103kg
Caps: 2
Points: 0

MATT BANAHAN

Club: Bath Rugby
Position: Wing/centre
Born: 30.12.86
Birthplace: St Brelade, Jersey

Height: 2.01m
Weight: 110kg
Caps: 2
Points: 10 - 2T

STEVE BORTHWICK

Club: Saracens
Position: Lock
Born: 12.10.79
Birthplace: Carlisle

Height: 1.96m
Weight: 114kg
Caps: 50
Points: 10 – 2T

DANNY CARE

Club: Harlequins
Position: Scrum Half
Born: 02.01.87
Birthplace: Leeds

Height: 1.74m
Weight: 84kg
Caps: 11
Points: 8 1T,DG

GEORGE CHUTER

Club: Leicester Tigers
Position: Hooker
Born: 09.07.76
Birthplace: Greenwich

Height: 1.78m
Weight: 96kg
Caps: 22
Points: 5 – 1T

TOM CROFT

Club: Leicester Tigers
Position: Flanker
Born: 07.11.85
Birthplace: Basingstoke

Height: 1.98m
Weight: 105kg
Caps: 13
Points: 0

MARK CUETO

Club: Sale Sharks
Position: Winger
Born: 26.12.79
Birthplace: Workington

Height: 1.83m
Weight: 95kg
Caps: 31
Points: 75 – 15T

LOUIS DEACON

Club: Leicester Tigers
Position: Lock
Born: 07.10.80
Birthplace: Leicester

Height: 1.98m
Weight: 115kg
Caps: 10
Points: 0

NICK EASTER

Club: Harlequins
Position: No 8
Born: 15.08.78
Birthplace: Epsom

Height: 1.93m
Weight: 114kg
Caps: 27
Points: 25 – 5T

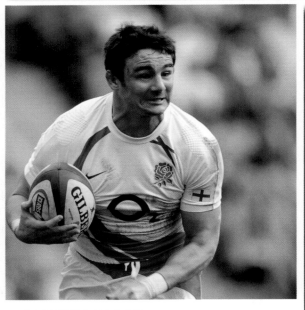

HARRY ELLIS

Club: Leicester Tigers
Position: Scrum half
Born: 17.05.82
Birthplace: Wigston

Height: 1.78m
Weight: 92kg
Caps: 27
Points: 25 –5T

TOBY FLOOD

Club: Leicester Tigers
Position: Fly half
Born: 08.08.85
Birthplace: Frimley

Height: 1.85m
Weight: 95kg
Caps: 26
Points: 62 – 3T, 7C, 10P, 1DP

RIKI FLUTEY

Club: London Wasps
Position: Centre
Born: 10.02.80
Birthplace: Wairarapa, New Zealand

Height: 1.79m
Weight: 93kg
Caps: 9
Points: 20 – 4T

ANDY GOODE

Club: AC Brive
Position: Fly half
Born: 03.04.80
Birthplace: Coventry

Height: 1.80
Weight: 95kg
Caps: 16
Points: 107 – 1T, 15C, 20P, 4DG

DYLAN HARTLEY

Club: Northampton Saints
Position: Hooker
Born: 24.03.86
Birthplace: Rotorua, New Zealand

Height: 1.85m
Weight: 109kg
Caps: 11
Points: 0

JAMES HASKELL

Club: London Wasps
Position: Flanker
Born: 02.04.85
Birthplace: Windsor

Height: 1.93m
Weight: 113kg
Caps: 19
Points: 0

BEN KAY

Club: Leicester Tigers
Position: Lock
Born: 14.12.75
Birthplace: Liverpool

Height: 1.96m
Weight: 117kg
Caps: 62
Points: 10 – 2T

TOM MAY

Club: Newcastle Falcons
Position: Centre
Born: 05.02.79
Birthplace: London

Height: 1.78m
Weight: 91kg
Caps: 2
Points: 0

LEE MEARS

Club: Bath Rugby
Position: Hooker
Born: 05.03.79
Birthplace: Torquay

Height: 1.73m
Weight: 96kg
Caps: 34
Points: 5 –1T

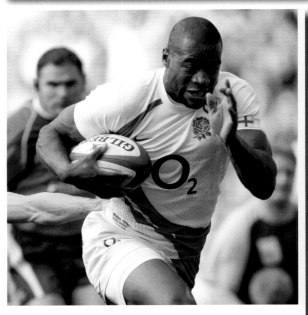

UGO MONYE

Club: Harlequins
Position: Wing
Born: 13.04.83
Birthplace: Islington

Height: 1.88m
Weight: 95kg
Caps: 6
Points: 5 – T

TOM PALMER

Club: London Wasps
Position: Lock
Born: 27.03.79
Birthplace: Haringey

Height: 1.99m
Weight: 113kg
Caps: 13
Points: 0

TIM PAYNE

Club: London Wasps
Position: Prop
Born: 29.04.79
Birthplace: Swindon

Height: 1.85m
Weight: 119kg
Caps: 12
Points: 0

CHRIS ROBSHAW

Club: Harlequins
Position: Back Row
Born: 04.06.86
Birthplace: Redhil

Height: 1.88m
Weight: 92kg
Caps: 1
Points: 0

PAUL SACKEY

Club: London Wasps
Position: Wing
Born: 08.11.79
Birthplace: Westminster

Height: 1.86m
Weight: 95kg
Caps: 22
Points: 55 – 11T

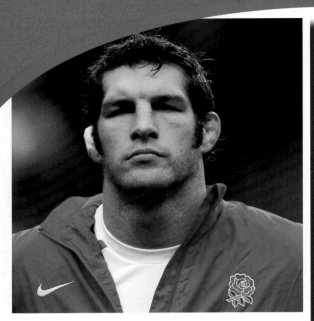

SIMON SHAW MBE

Club: London Wasps

Position: Lock

Born: 01.09.73

Birthplace: Nairobi, Kenya

Height: 2.03m

Weight: 123kg

Caps: 52

Points: 10 – 2T

ANDREW SHERIDAN

Club: Sale Sharks

Position: Prop

Born: 01.11.79

Birthplace: Bromley

Height: 1.93m

Weight: 117kg

Caps: 32

Points: 0

MATTHEW TAIT

Club: Sale Sharks

Position: Full back/centre

Born: 06.02.86

Birthplace: Shotley Bridge

Height: 1.83m

Weight: 94kg

Caps: 31

Points: 20 – 4T

MIKE TINDALL MBE

Club: Gloucester Rugby

Position: Centre

Born: 18.10.78

Birthplace: Otley

Height: 1.86m

Weight: 104kg

Caps: 60

Points: 69 – 13T, 2C

PHIL VICKERY MBE

Club: London Wasps
Position: Prop
Born: 14.03.76
Birthplace: Barnstaple

Height: 1.88m
Weight: 116kg
Caps: 73
Points: 10 – 2T

JULIAN WHITE MBE

Club: Leicester Tigers
Position: Prop
Born: 14.05.73
Birthplace: Plymouth

Height: 1.85m
Weight: 119kg
Caps: 51
Points: 0

JONNY WILKINSON OBE

Club: Toulon
Position: Fly half
Born: 25.05.79
Birthplace: Frimley

Height: 1.77m
Weight: 88kg
Caps: 70
Points: 1032 – 6T, 144C, 209P, 29DG

JOE WORSLEY

Club: London Wasps
Position: Back row
Born: 14.06.77
Birthplace: London

Height: 1.95m
Weight: 114kg
Caps: 72
Points: 50 – 10T

ANSWERS

SPOT THE DIFFERENCE (p.15)

WORDSEARCH (p.39)

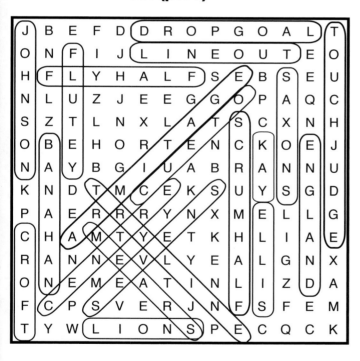

SPOT THE BALL (p.38)

QUIZ (p.16)

1. True
2. Bath
3. New Zealand
4. Jonny Wilkinson
5. Ireland, Scotland and Wales
6. Leicester Tigers
7. Steve Borthwick
8. False
9. Danny Care
10. False, he was born in New Zealand
11. Sydney
12. 16
13. 3
14. Sale Sharks
15. Leicester Tigers
16. Jason Robinson
17. True
18. Cardiff Blues
19. Dubai
20. Phil Vickery

GUESS WHO? (p.43)

1. Mark Cueto
2. Andrew Sheridan
3. Mike Tindall
4. Delon Armitage